How To
BALANCE
Your Life

Lead a successful life without neglecting your family, career and personal balance.

Alexandra Navarro

BALBOA.
PRESS
A DIVISION OF HAY HOUSE

www.theblueleaf.net

Editors:
Teri Taylor
Kelli Maeda

Author Photo:
Gina Prieto

Balboa Press books may be ordered through booksellers or by contacting:

Balboa Press
A Division of Hay House
1663 Liberty Drive
Bloomington, IN 47403
www.balboapress.com
1 (877) 407-4847

Printed in the United States of America.

ISBN: 978-1-4525-1857-2 (sc)
ISBN: 978-1-4525-1858-9 (e)

Balboa Press rev. date: 11/04/2014

CONTENTS

Learn to Visualize

Trust Your Intuition

Dedication

This book is dedicated to you, yes to you! I desire that you receive all the guidance and support necessary to inspire your life, achieve your goals, and reach optimal growth within your spirit, heart and soul.

Introduction

As a woman, mother of three, wife, and professional, I often think about my role within the communities that I belong to and how I can choose to be a driving force behind positive change for future generations.

It is my belief that we all have "the power within" to positively influence our own lives and the world around us. I am personally committed to helping make tomorrow's world a better place, which serves as a constant source of daily joy and fulfillment.

Here are my core values, which guide me on a daily basis:

- *We are all the "architects" of our own reality and co creators with God of the world* we live in. We all have the power to choose to live a life with purpose and create our own experience.
- *We all have the same possibility of achieving our dreams and goals*, no matter what challenges or unexpected events life holds for us. All dreams are possible for us, whether it be finding a life partner, pursuing the career of our dreams, or living a healthy life style.
- *We can all find serenity and balance in everything that life brings us.* Practicing "daily balance" in one's actions

invites positive change on a larger scale. To create daily balance, I take time to walk on the beach, meditate, think positively, live healthy, and am grateful for all that is good in my life. I am passionate about my family, my work, dancing and traveling.

This book invites you to find your power from within and become the architect of your own reality, to pursue your dreams and goals, and find true serenity and balance for your life.

I invite you to use this book as a daily guide and refereance. It is full or practical tips and techniques that you can start applying in your daily life today.

I introduce the principles of harmony, balance, and iintuitive flow with a simple and practical approach. My request is for you to invite these principles into every aspect of your being.

I will share my collection of experience while working with high level executives from leading corporations and individuals in the health and well-being industry.

Apply these steps of transformation and you will find yourself becoming a conscience leader in your business, within your community, and foremost deep within yourself.

I invite you to share a moment of your journey with me, to free yourself from any charges of the past, and allow your dreams to come true.

Alexandra Navarro
Founder of The Blue Leaf

Invitations for the Week

Each week, you are invited to select 3 of the goals below:

- Drink 6-8 glasses of water per day.
- Breathe: Set a reminder to do deep breathing exercises once a day.
- Write down your goals and put them in a visible place.
- Exchange negative thoughts for positive thoughts.
- Be present with your family, friends, and yourself.
- Identify the emotions of the person whom you are with.
- Organize your space. Give away, donate, or plan a garage sale to get rid of clothes and belongings you do not use any more.
- Commune with nature: Find 15 minutes to spend in nature every day. Watch a sunset or a sunrise and dawn break. Bring this energy into your hands and put it into your heart.
- Become more aware of your surroundings. Take notice of great things in nature... animals, trees, and all living beings. Allow yourself to be inspired by all of that.
- Focus on staying grounded.
- Tune in with your inner wisdom, become close to God, ask a question, and listen.
- Meditate to relax and to develop your conection with our inner wisdom. You can listen to relaxing meditations.

- Eat a balanced meal for breakfast. Check to see that every morning you are eating a variety of fruits and protein. My favorite breakfast foods are: granola & chopped fruit with yogurt, and one egg.
- Listen to relaxing music for one hour every day. Some suggestions are Enya or sounds of nature.
- Exercise at least 30 minutes per day, three times per week.

Starting on One's Path

It is very easy to get confused about what one truly "wants" and what one is "expected" to do in this lifetime. This question was precisely what helped me to get clarity for the life path, which I am now on...

In 2007, I graduated in Management from a University in Silicon Valley California, USA. Completing two degrees was quite significant for me. Firstly at attaining one of my personal goals, as I have always been a lover of knowledge. Secondly, creating a segue into the corporate world where I later spent time in my career as an executive, after taking a few years off with my second child.

The moment I touched the paper of my diploma, I felt a great sense of pride and happiness, and yet at the same time, a sense of uncertainty about what my future would hold. In the days that followed this period of my life, I found was asking myself some much 'bigger' questions:

- What am I really supposed to be doing with my life?
- What is my mission in life?
- What about my family? What about my personal interests? How will I be able to manage everything?

It is when I started to ask myself and reflect upon these very questions, that I was empowered to choose my path and begin to exercise my full personal leadership...

RECONNECTING & TUNING
INTO THE FLOW

"The problems are not people, places, and situations,
but rather the thoughts of them."

- Dr. Ihaleakala Hew Len, PhD

Conscious Leaders

When things work out smoothly and effortlessly, we often call it "being in the flow."

In times of great change within our economic, social, environmental, and family lives, companies demand balanced leaders who know how to make innovative and forward-thinking decisions. As executives, businesspeople, students, and employees, we must achieve these goals without overlooking the other important aspects of our personal lives, such as being a parent, friend, son/daughter, or any other role, while being ourselves and feeling happy and fulfilled by our activities.

Being a leader is achievable for everyone who sets his or her mind to it. We are facing a global leadership crisis; high-level executives, for example, are under great pressure to guide their organizations towards higher and higher goals. This can lead to the disregard of their well-being, which is not just disastrous for their companies but also brings those executives unsatisfactory personal lives that have an end result in "burn-out."

According to Harvard's Business School, today's ideal leader must possess not only professional balance but also create balance in 5 areas of their life: intellectual, financial, social, emotional, and spiritual.

In the process of understanding these levels of balance, you will develop your ability to reach your higher potential, cultivate internal strength, and become a Balanced Leader.

I use the word "Leader" to refer to all people who are executives, business people, independent professionals, parents, students, and all those who lead any role or activity that requires balance.

When I use the term "Balance," I am referring to the stability we encounter during times of change or transition.

We will take into account very simple and important aspects in order for you to regain Balance in your life and become a Balanced Leader.

Let's take a closer look at the 5 levels that a Conscious Leader must incorporate, and understand what will happen when these 5 aspects are combined.

Physical Aspect

Our physical body is an instrument at our service. We want to respect it, take care of it, listen to it, and keep it healthy, it is our means of survival on this planet.

Case: 'Diana'

One of my clients, 'Diana,' shared with me that when we started working together she exercised every day at the gym. When I asked her what she had for breakfast, she told me she always has a coffee, a donut, and if time, a slice of pineapple. And when I asked her how much time she spent outdoors, she told me that although she lives in a wonderful place by the sea, she only goes to the beach occasionally because she has so little time.

We talked about the importance of viewing our physical body as an instrument at our service, which deserves our attention and care each day. Diana continues to exercise daily, which is ideal. She has changed her breakfast menu and now drinks 6-8 glasses of water a day. She organizes her time better to take 15 minutes of each morning to see the sunrise. This was enough for her to feel calmer.

Emotional Aspect

Emotions are the way we respond to events - they are neither bad nor good. We cannot see them, can we? But we feel them.

How many emotions do we have in a day or in a week? How many of them are positive? How many times a day do we find ourselves irritated, anxious, stressed, happy, sad? How many of our emotions allow us to stay in "the flow"?

It is okay to feel; it is okay to love: it is okay to cry. What we have to shift are the existing feelings of sadness, anguish, anxiety, or irritability that we experience too often.

Blue Leaf

Depression, sadness, and irritability block our energy flow. When we are upset we are not vibrating at the creativity or productivity level, therefore it becomes normal in our day-to-day life for things to not work out the way we want them to.

If, for example, today you feel irritable or depressed, it is important to acknowledge these feelings, and above all, to accept them. By bringing an awareness of your mental state to your consciousness, you relieve half of the problem. You want to avoid censoring your feelings. The solution to this staged control is not by removing our feelings but accepting them, respecting them, and being accountable for them so that we can come into complete Balance and be healed.

We have to allow ourselves to experience feelings completely; otherwise, they may cause us a lot of trouble and manifest in our lives on mental, physical, and spiritual levels. Healing your emotions is a very important part of the process of healing on a physical level.

Case: Myself

I have lived away from my country for over 10 years; being away from my roots, my parents, my language, and my culture, I used to get depressed often. I felt alone and sometimes angry with myself for having left my country. These feelings became regular and I was not able to solve them. I was in a vicious cycle.

Little by little, I understood that many of my feelings could be changed. For example, I learned that when I got irritable, it was better to accept the emotion and apply the wise advice, *"one is the owner of his own thoughts…"* and go for a walk on the beach so that I could consciously change how I was feeling, while doing an activity that I enjoyed.

Listening to nature sounds and music, applying drops of essential oils such as olive, jasmine, or rose behind the ears, and using Bach Floral Essences helped me change my mood so that I could regain control of my emotions.

Remember you create things that happen later.

Mental Aspect

Intellect is our mental level, the skills we use to think and reason. It is made up of thoughts, attitudes, beliefs and values.

Since an early age, we have acquired other people's beliefs about what is right and wrong. However, many of these beliefs may cause confusion and lead us to down the wrong path, even if it feels like the right one.

Case Study: Nicky

My client 'Nicky,' the director of a recognized technology enterprise, felt that nothing in her life was turning out right. She had divorced two years ago, and still was not over her ex-husband. She thought life made no sense and that she would not be able to raise her children. At work, she did not feel valued enough, and had just missed out on an opportunity to be promoted. On top of that, she felt guilty for not spending enough time with her children who were still very young. When I asked her to count how many negative thoughts she had for one week, we concluded that over 75% of her thoughts were negative.

Picture yourself waking up and getting out of bed after the alarm has rung. You have been awakened out of a really deep sleep

- *rrrrriiinnnggg!* The first moment of the day's stress enters your body the second you wake up. What is the first thing that comes to your mind? Then, you go into the shower but you have forgotten to fix the water heater, so you have to take a shower with freezing water. And there comes the second thought of "Arghhh!" (We'll call all those negative thoughts "Arghhh!").

Let's carry on with your day. You eat breakfast in a hurry, thinking that you do not have enough time to get to work. Then there is the daily traffic to battle. Next you run out of gas, and then you arrive late to the office. Of course your boss is in a grumpy mood. What time is it? Maybe 9 am, right? How many negative thoughts have you had already?

If we continue in our busy day and do not have time to see your children, or go to a concert you wanted to see, or study for your exam… you realize that accumulation of these negative thoughts keep us from "flowing". This blockage does not allow us to become conscious; don't let your thoughts keep you away from your desires!

Start by becoming aware of your feelings, then capture them and change your thoughts to positive ones. It works!

I started my own changing process when I was pregnant with Federico, my first son. I used to judge myself as unattractive, while I thought my pregnant friends all looked perfect. I had similar thoughts at work; I thought I was doing everything wrong…. And guess what? By holding this negative energy I attracted to myself more unhappiness, instead of enjoying the most precious moments that a woman can have.

Every time I had a negative thought, I caught myself by saying: *"Oops, negative thought on board!"* And then I would say out loud: *"I choose to create positive thoughts."*

Even if you are having the worst day, and anybody can have them... just remember that shifting your negative thoughts immediately will change your awareness. Letting go of your negative thoughts will release this stuck energy and get you back into the flow.

Spiritual Aspect

This aspect is related to our connection, to our inner wisdom; in my case (in this book), I will make reference towards God. In the society in which we live, it is common to feel too much intellectual and material pressure. Disconnecting from our essence is easy and then we start feeling empty and lost, as though we have no destination for our life.

Unconsciously, we seek happiness in money, power, and success. We fall into acceptable addictive behaviors such as; overeating, being workaholics, abusing alcohol, compulsive shoppers, or gambling. These are things that make us feel alive and only disguise the pain we are feeling. Sooner or later we discover that none of these methods are effective in filling the gaps that caused the disconnection from our inner wisdom, God.

When we learn to balance our emotions, our body, and our mind spirituality, our inner wisdom begins to show itself. And if we accept God's help, we realize we are not alone. Each of us is part of the same consciousness. We are all part of the same whole, and when we keep a clear conscience, following our intuition is much easier.

A Balanced Leader will experience balance on an intellectual, financial, emotional, and spiritual level.

Make Your Goals, Be Ready for Change

With this new perception, awareness and understanding of theses different aspects in our life that need growth, we can now choose to create Balance. We are ready to initiate change.

Now you are ready for change, and have decided to take charge of your life, or you simply know that something inside you has to change. Let's start with a question. Ask yourself: What do I wish for? What do I want to achieve? How do I want to feel? Write it down.

Write down your principal goal. For example: *"Feeling peaceful and happy again. Regain Balance in my life. Finding purpose in my life."*

Now that you have a clear principal goal, using these 5 fundamental elements, decide what you truly want for your life

- Professional goal
- Spiritual goal
- Physical goal
- Relationship goal
- Financial goal

There is no need for you to write them all. If you only want to achieve one, that is fine. Feel it from the bottom of your heart, without thinking. Do it now.

Case Study: Mario

When Mario began his process, here are the goals he wrote down:

- Professional goal: Being accepted by my co-workers.
- Spiritual goal: Deepen the connection with my spirituality.
- Physical goal: Losing weight.

- Relationship goal: None.
- Financial goal: None.

Mario did not write something for all the goals. Just ask yourself what would make you feel happy. It can be something specific if that is what you want.

Mario's results after 8 weeks were the following: *He got a promotion at work, and his co-workers were talking to him in a different way, taking him into account in relevant decisions for the company. He read 4 books on spiritual growth; in turn, he began to listen to his voice and intuition and developed self-confidence. And he lost 26 lbs in 8 weeks!*

During the process, Mario added a new goal: improve the relationship he had with his wife. He is still working on that one, and he understands many lessons with his wife while being present in the moment.

I have personally worked with 100's of people, and in all cases there has been positive progress and achievements after an average of six sessions.

The graph below shows the evolution of clients regarding the principal goal they set after 6 sessions.

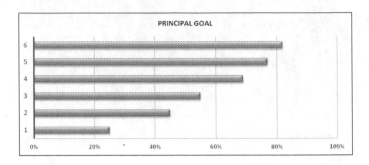

Note: Bar 4 represents the average progress achieved by each of the clients during the training at the beginning of each session. 82% of the clients reached a level of Balance after 6 sessions. This illustration puts together a sample of over 400 participants between 2007 and 2010, using the Blue Leaf Methodology.

Now that you have understanding with the concept of Balance and have written down your purpose, we will remove and clear any existing negative thoughts energy. For this, I invite you to read the following meditation slowly and in a quiet place. Put it into practice!

Social Aspect

This aspect represents how we communicate with others. Here the acceptance of vulnerability is developed as an aspect that makes us stronger as leaders, including the recognition of error as a critical point to innovation. In my next book we will go more in-depth to the social aspect.

Reconnecting & Tuning Into the Flow Meditation

~

Look for a peaceful place. Take a position that is comfortable. You can sit down with your feet on the floor.

Close your eyes.

Imagine yourself in a quiet place where you have access to an abundance of nature. Try to envision as many details as you can in that natural space.

Breathe slowly and deeply.

Now visualize a light that surrounds and protects you.

Focus on breathing slowly and deeply. Remember, breathing is how you connect with your awareness and consciousness.

Visualize yourself letting go of all the energy you do not need anymore.

Breathe slowly and deeply.

Give thanks for this moment and feel the difference inside you.

Open your eyes and breathe again slowly and deeply.

FORGIVING & RELEASING

"Resentment is like drinking poison and then
hoping it will kill your enemies."

- Nelson Mandela

Organization is the Product of Your Clear Intention

When we organize the space in which we live, we are opening and moving energy so that we can receive new things, and we are unblocking energy that cannot flow.

Organization is the product of your clear intentions. You may have too many responsibilities that leave you with no time to breathe or space to think.

Disorder and unfinished business is blocked energy! It is important to keep order at home, at work, even in our closets, so we can keep inner Balance.

Keep Your Life Simple

The simpler you keep your life, and the fewer unneeded things you accumulate, the happier you will be. One of my teachers and spiritual guide says that every 6 months it is very important to review all of our possessions, and sell or donate things we have not used for a year or more. Surely, someone else needs what we do not, and by keeping these items we are blocking ourselves from being in the flow.

Case: A TV Show Donation

In a TV show a long time ago, I saw how someone called to request a wheelchair for her daughter who could not walk because of an accident she had at the age of three. A few minutes later there was a call from a lady offering a wheelchair in perfect condition. She was invited to deliver it in person and then interviewed in the program. To my surprise, the lady was crying. She realized that the 12-year-old girl had not been out of her house to see the light of day. Her mother, being single

and poor, worked all day, so the girl had to crawl to feed herself. Of course when the new wheelchair came to the house the girl left the neighborhood for a "walk." That was enough to make her happy.

The donator said that she had the chair stored in the garage for over 12 years! Her husband had used it before dying and she had kept it as memory.

Let's not accumulate things as a memory. We do not know how badly others might need these physical things. We will still have our memories.

My husband and I do a thorough deep cleaning of our house two times per year, including drawers, closets and the garage. We look at this cleaning as an opportunity to distribute belongings that are in good condition and that we no longer use to people who are in need and can really use them. Sometimes we will host a garage sale and use the proceeds towards an event such as our annual "100 Children Receiving Santa," which is where we have Christmas presents delivered to children internationally.

When I talk to my clients and ask them to organize their wardrobes, they are surprised, we don't realize how significant this exercise is for our minds. The results of this task are incredible. In particular, arranging furniture and organizing our shoes help keep us grounded. One client of mine, an extremely creative and intelligent woman who was an executive of a technology enterprise at the time, had a hard time asking for a raise. She knew she deserved it, but making money for her talents, which she considered a gift, was not easy for her. When I asked about her wardrobe, she told me it was a mess, and that she put her shoes on hangers in the middle of her closet. I requested that she sort, straighten up and organize her clothes, and also for her to arrange the shoes that she uses on the floor of her closet.

A few weeks later she called to tell me that she had had a meeting with her boss. She requested the pay raise and it was granted without any questions asked.

Cleaning at all levels of your life is very important. Removing the old, and focusing on the next steps for your life. Check to see what unnecessary baggage you may be holding onto from the past, when you are released of these things and get rid of them, you will see how the energy re-aligns and begins to flow again.

Take a Moment to Relax

Case: My Being Lost

Many years ago, after having my daughter, Daniela, I decided to take break from my job and be a full-time mother. Of course, with chores to do, two babies to care for, and no family help, I was extremely tired. My husband worked very hard, traveled a lot with his job, and worked part time with a relative for his exporting company. We constantly had friends and family visiting for holiday, because we lived in such a lovely destination spot.

After a few month of attempting to be a super professional, super wife, and super friend I found myself very sick. I was completely exhausted, overwhelmed and lost sight of where my life was headed, and what my life's purpose was.

After several months in that state and having doctors run several tests that luckily turned out normal, I decided to take a close look at myself and ask for help.

At that time my husband's job required us to relocate to California and we moved in a matter of weeks. That, of course, added more work for me because he had to travel before we moved. My mom and dad came to help with the children and the move. After several sleepless nights we arrived in California to a beautiful ocean front city.

For our first few weeks, these were no visiting the beach. I focused on resting up and trying to reconnect but with little success. My children being ages 1 and 2 required all of my attention, but I could not give it to them. So I decided to take a few days off. At this point I did not know if I wanted to continue living in the United States, where my family had a great life. I wondered: What about me? My husband is a person who likes sports, is focused, intelligent, and lovely, but he could only help me in the evenings, as long as he wasn't too tired for work the following day. We only had a few minutes of dialogue when he arrived home, and I felt I was getting no downtime. We started losing our partnership, our way of being creative and expressing our being. We were just getting by day to day.

The moments of joy had fallen away significantly and had been replaced by routine, work, work, and more work. What had happened to us? From the outside, our family and friends saw a perfect setting: happy marriage, two beautiful children, and a great husband. Apparently, we were happy and calm but I felt absolutely miserable. Our lives were running so fast.

Federico, my oldest son, was extremely hyperactive. He did not stay still for a second but he spoke to me with his eyes. I swear he scolded me and almost bossed me around! I have always known he is a special being. My heart understood that Federico's actions were because he could not express himself due to his limited vocabulary at his young age. With his eyes, he expressed everything that he felt. He could not tell me he was acting like that because he felt the tension we had at home, the sadness of my heart, and that the energy of our home was extremely low. He simply could not express it. My husband and I were the ones taking away his peace. Our energy broke his harmony, and resulted in him feeling chaos and acting out hyperactivity.

Case: My Getting "Found" in Brazil

When I arrived to Brazil, a friend of my brother-in-law was waiting for me at the airport. He took me to my hotel. I was too confused to start re-evaluating my life and what I wanted from it. All I could think about were the multiple activities I had, the little help I felt from my family, the responsibility of raising my children, and the lack of focus and perspective I had over my life goals.

When the sun came up in Brazil, in the city of Rio Negro, away from home, away from my husband, away from my children, and far away from the drama, I realized how our of Balance my life was and that I had to do something. My son was telling me so with his 'behavior.' His young being and soul were trying to draw attention to the need for change and trying to help me. I went to see what activities I could do in the small town where I was staying. I decided to go on a boat tour that went around Rio Negro for 6 hours. I wanted to explore and know where I was.

We left at 10 a.m. The sun was glorious and there were only three people on the boat, including the captain. I was thrilled watching the river, which is extremely large and one of the most beautiful places I have ever known. A few hours later a thunderstorm came that made us lose our way. There was almost no visibility.

We were lost for several hours, searching for the right way. When the rain finally stopped, the boat was full of water and everyone's cellphones were damaged and we had somehow run out of gas! The only thing we could do was wait for another boat to appear to take us ashore. A few hours passed and while I waited, I had the opportunity to get to know the other two people that were with me. We talked for a while and enjoyed nature.

"Look, look," said the captain. *"Let's make signs asking that boat passing by in the distance to help us."* We tried to get the their attention, but as far away as we were, the people aboard the other boat could not see us.

Finally, around 6 pm, a small raft passed by us but it could not take us to the city because it did not have any gasoline and only used diesel, which did not serve us either. The small raft towed us to a nearby shore, where we found a seemingly deserted beach, but there were many natives on shore. We were greeted with kindness and two of them went in search of gasoline. Meanwhile, the tribe was trying to communicate with us and make our short stay enjoyable. At that time we did not know how long we would stay there. The simplicity of their lives amazed me. Their food, ceremonies, and the words of their leader did too: ***"Remember to dance and do whatever makes you happy."*** I do not know why he said it. He just did and then left.

The sunset was splendid. The Amazon region is famous for its sunsets and pink dolphins among other things. I had the opportunity to see and enjoy the dolphins that afternoon. Near midnight, the gas finally arrived and we could return to town safely.

I can still remember this wonderful experience with the sunset and the dolphins and see it in my mind. I listened to the tribe leader's voice inside my heart over and over. Life has to change! I needed to re-establish Balance in my life. *I needed to work on myself, dance with the flow of life and do what really made me happy.* I understood.

Work and challenges will always be there. We can choose to create opportunities and see life in other colors. Focus on what is really necessary and stop trying to do too much at once, take time to relax. Enjoy your children to the fullest. Find time to exist alone and/or as a couple. And above all, find a place, and a moment to experience peace of mind and find who you really are. Take the time to feel, smell, and listen to your inner voice and to be aligned in harmony with yourself.

We all need time to rest, time to have fun, and time to love. My experience in Brazil was the beginning of my inner healing. I actually had time and space to reconsider my priorities, goals, and values.

Travel Lightly; Forgive & Accept

In the process of finding Balance, you must learn to 'forgive and accept' any past 'wrongs,' **cast** away all the negative thoughts and actions that you no longer need, and see what lessons and opportunities a balanced life can present to you.

Healing your life starts when you stop living through your emotions and start living from your heart. It starts when you remember compassion and respect toward others. *Remember this: When you vibrate from the energy of love, acceptance and healing follow.*

There are many exercises that we can do to help us forgive, but the true magic begins when we bring our emotions into consciousness, and then allow them to reside where we feel most peaceful. Then, forgiveness is simple. Our grudges change first into acceptance, and then to compassion, and finally they go away.

Part of this process is to stop listening to your internal critic. We have an internal voice that makes negative comments about things we do and tells us we are doing things wrong. This voice says things like, *"You do not deserve it,"* or *"You are not capable of doing that."* This voice is capable of making our every day lives miserable. Being aware of this voice can help us heal.

Listening to the internal critic becomes habit. To heal the emotional damage that this voice brings, we have to accept our past, and our wounds that have likely been with us since childhood.

Trying to forget the past can be complicated. Can it be done? Most certainly it can, although you will not see progress by stuffing away past experiences that have not yet been resolved in your life.

It is time to put aside all the hurt of your inner child. It is time to release your anger and despair and begin a healing process with acceptance.

It is not always necessary to talk to someone in person to obtain the desired result of forgiveness. Each situation is different. For example, writing a long letter in which you honestly explain your feelings, or simply sharing your meditation with this person and letting them know everything you want are two ways of approaching forgiveness. Of course, if you feel the urge to talk with this person, to have a heart to heart and clarify the past, then by all means do it.

The people we cannot forgive could be showing us mirrors. You are the result of the choices you make. Those situations, which have had consequences in your childhood, are perhaps the most painful and uncomfortable ones to revisit. They are not the result of true values. When we consciously choose situations, we create satisfactory living conditions.

Love is not Abuse

When you realize how simple this concept is, you will see all the people in your life differently. No one will scare you. They might all keep the same position and the same attitude, but you will see them differently.

Start by remembering those who helped you grow up. Surely everything they chose at that moment was based on their priorities and not on yours.

Case: My Mother & I

When my first son, Federico, was born, my mom helped us care for the baby. She stayed with us for a month. She cooks delicious food, is great to talk to, and is a loving kind person.

Usually when my husband came home from work, we went to the pool, and he and my mom had a glass of wine and chatted for a while. Like that, days passed and I believed everything was fine. One day, my husband asked me why I did not spend more time bonding with my mother. I always waited for him to arrive before offering her a snack or sharing time with her in the pool. Truth be told, I had not noticed that I was avoiding my mother, so I searched inside for the reason, **"the why"** for this situation, and asked myself, what was I supposed to understand?

Shortly after exploring **"the reason"** of my conversation with my husband about my mother, I let my intuition flow and realized that in my childhood I was very rebellious. I still remember and think, "How embarrassing!" But the rebellion within me was because I wanted to do different things. There was unfairness that hurt me and over time it accumulated more and more. When my mother scolded me, I did not know how to explain what I wanted and, of course, she did not understand. She was doing from her heart the best she could do.

I created the forgiveness exercise that you will do in a moment. I revisited my childhood and realized that what my mom gave me was her very best with all her heart, deep within her intuition, and above all the best according to our situation. I asked her to forgive me for not telling her how much I love her as often as I should, for judging her, for not understanding, and for all that I thought had been wrong in my life, but was actually not wrong.

After all, what I thought was wrong are actually the lessons that built the person I am today.

The relationship with my mother changed completely when I had Daniela, my second child. Again, my Mom came to help us, and we spent a fabulous time together swimming at the pool, talking, and just enjoying our time together.

Understanding the real content of the mirror I had since my childhood helped me get closer to my dreams, rather than being judgmental or fear of talking to someone about it, regardless of who they are in my life. I remembered that we are all equal, and then, love towards my inner self also began to grow.

Forgiveness & Acceptance are the Best Unblocking Tools

In every instance of your life, forgiveness helps you free yourself and helps you become who you really are.

If you live in the past and according to old rules, it is almost impossible to forgive. All of your past experiences are positive if you see them as stepping-stones to help you grow spiritually. When you really forgive from the heart, you are able to see any relationship in your life with the eyes of your own being, as well as through the eyes of someone else. You will see the lessons that each person teaches you. **When you forgive, you will see the other with the soul's eyes.**

You will discover yourself getting closer to you inner wisdom and start seeing everything from a different perspective. You will start to understand who you truly are. And, believe me, your true self already has the ability to guide you in your life. You will start seeing the past without feeling like a victim, and there will be a true transformation in your life.

From today forward, remember and repeat this in your mind: **"I am the only creator and wholly responsible for the reality I live in. I build my own happiness."**

Case: 'Lorena'

Lorena made an appointment with me because she was completely torn apart. Her boyfriend had broken up with her. Their relationship was pretty stressful and she did not know what to do.

She had a very strict boss; she smoked too much and cried often. Lorena did not feel capable of ending her relationship or doing anything on her own. After a few sessions in where we focused on becoming conscious and the importance of living in balance, forgiving herself, forgiving the person who had hurt her, and understanding the lessons her boyfriend and her boss were trying to mirror, she found clarity. Her boyfriend did not respect her because she did not respect herself; she judged herself constantly and felt like a victim. By merely bringing awareness of these feelings into her consciousness, she learned to respect herself and no longer felt like a victim.

Lorena's life completely changed. In a few months she found a new job. She got into the university she had always dreamed of working at after being a student there, and she put a peaceful end to her relationship.

Lorena consciously understood that she was in denial about the abuse that this person was causing her. The problem I saw was that her soul was trying to teach her to love, respect, and value herself at some level. She needed to see herself with the soul's eyes and learn to accept this love and support.

Today, Lorena is ready to start a new romantic relationship and she is happy in her new job. Through forgiveness and acceptance she has found peace, despite her feeling like she could never achieve it. ***Remember there is always the possibility of healing and growth.***

Lorena shows us that it is with forgiveness that we are able to move and take a step forward. We can see that the more we have been hurt, the more compassionate we can be. ***To accept means to value and see with the soul's eyes the lessons that life wants to teach us. This is how we are able to move on and make growth.***

Forgiveness and acceptance are actions that break the mind and soul barriers. When the barriers are removed, you will realize who you truly are. This is when you can begin to receive and experiment with new perspective. You will also start to realize that this life is like taking a part in a theatre play, where your friends and family are part of the same show.

At the end, when masks and costumes come off, you will see their true souls and only then, you will understand the meaning and content of the play. This is your play; this is your life.

Forgiveness Exercise

Choose 3 people that you love; they can be a family memeber, friend or relative. Now write down 4 good qualites and 4 flaws for each of these individuals.

Name: _____

Qualities	Flaws
* _____	* _____
* _____	* _____
* _____	* _____
* _____	* _____

Name: _____

Qualities	Flaws
* _____	* _____
* _____	* _____
* _____	* _____
* _____	* _____

Name: _____

Qualities	Flaws
* _____	* _____
* _____	* _____
* _____	* _____
* _____	* _____

Now do the same exercise, but this time with a person you do not like so much, someone who has hurt you deeply:

Meditation & Forgiveness

Look for a quiet place. As soon as you wake up or at night before going to bed are the best moments to do this exercise. Place a piece of paper and a pencil beside you. Take a position that is comfortable. You can sit down with your feet on the floor or lie down with a pillow under your knees for support.

Close your eyes and start breathing slowly and deeply. Inhale a few times and exhale slowly after each inhalation. Relax your body, release your muscles, and relax as deeply as you can.

Take another deep breath and, while you exhale, calm your mind and let your thoughts go.

When new thoughts come into your head, let them go easily, and allow your mind to stay calm, gradually and slowly, until you feel peaceful inside.

Now imagine a place filled with nature. Visualize a cottage or a warm house within that natural environment. Inside the house imagine you are with people from the past, and repeat with your inner voice:

Name: _____

I Forgive You for:

_____

_____

I Ask You Forgiveness for:

_____

_____

Thank You for Teaching me:

_____

_____

And you will say to him/her:

"(*Name of the person*), I give you forgiveness, and ask you to forgive me."

At the end, ask your Inner Child to forgive you.

When you feel calm and sure that all emotions are quelled, return consciously to the place you visualized and become aware of your body again. Feel that which is around you. When you are ready, open your eyes, stretch, and breathe slowly and deeply.

You will remember more people as the weeks go on. Friends, relatives, anyone… Do the same exercise: "I forgive you and ask for your forgiveness."

How do you feel now?

LIVING IN THE PRESENT

"We cannot be in the present while longing for the past...
one has to let go and detach."

- **Paulo Coelho**

Over time I learned that it is very important to live each moment feeling balanced, calm, and satisfied. Every day I value what I do, and I feel excited by my own happiness, by doing this, I can really give all I have.

I give my best to my husband, my children, my parents, my career, and my friends. This is the premise by which I live my life.

Quality not Quantity: The quantity of hours that I share with my three children is not as important as the quality of time I can give them. My best gift is to be "present," sharing 100% of myself with them. Working is also part of me, so when I work, I enjoy my profession. The true challenge is to be entirely present in each moment, while enjoying, sharing, or giving of myself in every situation.

Change Begins within Me and Depends on Me: It took courage to start exploring who I really was: the good, the bad, what I want, and what I need. I constantly observed my thoughts and changed my old beliefs, which did not allow me to be positive or support my present or future.

Each morning after breathing deeply and thanking God for a new day, I repeat out loud: ***"I deserve the best. I accept that."***

Positive thoughts and emotions work together. They create my reality and that depends soley on me.

Focus: Having my children by my side while thinking about email to be answered, and being at work and thinking about picking up my children on time from school made me feel disconnected from the place where I really had to be. Now I have play-dates with my children, and I ask for help in my work every time I need it. I understand that I cannot do everything on my own. This has helped me to be present with my children as well as become an excellent professional.

Some days are better than others, but I am always practicing awareness and being alert. When frustration or anger come into my mind, I breathe deeply and focus on the moment I am living. Believe me, everyone benefits. Having focus and the ability to be present affects each member of my family and absolutely everything I do. Being present within my heart is a routine practical question too. These tools make all the difference.

Being Aware of the World that Surround Us

Let us begin by trying to be more aware of what is in our surroundings. This is possible when we stop for a moment and lower the intensity of our daily activities, breathe, and pay attention.

When you go to work, for example, look at what surrounds you. Look at the setting, try to feel nature, notice the sky. Really observe what is around you. Focus on the present; on the moment you are in. Do not stay in the past or in the future, be "just right here and now."

Usually we do not live in the moment because we are attached to the past or thinking about the future. When you are on your way to the office, notice if you are constantly thinking about whether you are going to arrive late, that your boss is going to get angry, that the traffic is horrible, etc.

When I arrived to the U.S.A., I thought about Colombia all the time and this went on for many years. It was supposed to be a normal part of the adaptation process during the first year. The strange thing was that over a year went by and my thoughts were still stuck on my family, my friends, and my old job. I was not enjoying my new life; I was living in the past and in the future, but not in the present. I was clearly not accepting the lessons that life was giving me according to what I had asked for. I continued to feel regret, lonely, sad and cry often. It wasn't until I realized what was happening, that I could actually allow myself to feel supported. For the first time ever I began to use my senses by connecting with Nature, surrounding myself with awesome people. I would sit in different places of nature for at least five minutes each day. For example, some days I sat and enjoyed the sunrise, other days I simply observed a tree at the park. When I could, I loved to go to the ocean, a close by river, or into the woods.

Now it is Your Turn

Notice what is around you. Make your senses aware. Go somewhere in nature. What do you see? What do you hear? What do you smell? What do you feel? Where are you? At first, your senses will surely resist, but after some days of practice you will see the result, and you will begin to be conscious of what surrounds you. You will **be present**.

Understand How Others Affect You

The character of people and spaces that surround us do affect us. If we learn to be present, we will know how to carry ourselves.

For example, I require the sun to work and feel alive, even if only for a few minutes each day. Otherwise, after a couple of weeks I feel depressed and drained. It took a long time for me to come to an understanding of this. It was while I was working for an import company that I started to feel very uncomfortable within myself. I was very inpatient, felt annoyed by many things around me, and without consciously understanding how... I was absorbing the problems of the people who were working with and around me, which was affecting me greatly.

When I am conscious to sensing what people reflect, I can experience the mood of those who surround me. I now can read peoples mood and most importantly know how to prevent it from negatively affecting me. By understanding how to deal with the mood of those around me, I know how to react when difficult situations arise. By having this awareness and conscience practice, I can prevent myself from being drained by others.

Being present and conscious of people who are in my close surroundings allows me to control my own well being. I can feel their emotions, yet I am not affected by it.

In the company of a friend or stranger, anytime you are with someone, breathe slowly and deeply while you are interacting. Once you exhale, concentrate on his/her mood. Check to see what you feel within you. What does this person trigger in you?

- Calmness
- Discomfort
- Nervousness
- Relaxation

You do not have to be listening to this person to notice his/her mood. Notice what you feel:

- Calmness
- Happiness
- Sadness

- Learning
- Anger
- Discomfort

You can do the same exercise with the places you frequently visit. Maybe you feel happy always going to a particular place, or maybe you avoid another place because it does not offer tranquility.

Know that if you feel your inner strength being drained, you have options. Remember that it is always important to be present and conscious to feel better. For example, you can simply leave the place you are in. Do not classify it as bad or good. Instead recognize that it just does not fit your needs. You can cut off a conversation or redirect it. Many people drain your energy without you even noticing. They are called "vampires," because while they are telling you their problems or their anecdotes they are draining your inner strength. At the end of the conversation you might feel as if you just spoke in an auditorium in front of a million people. If you are aware, having your inner strength drained will be easier to control.

I recall a situation that happened with one of my cousins. It was over a summer vacation at her house, when we would leave for work together every morning. I would drop her off and then continue on to my work. When I arrived at the office, it was 8 o'clock in the morning, and I was already tired. After two weeks of this, I noticed that my cousin always told me her sad stories and problems on the way to work. But the serious part was that she always saw a negative horizon, or she simply did not see any solution. So I had wasted the hour trying to make her see opportunities and talking about what I felt without noticing what was happening. Now I understand that when you try to share your feelings with loved ones, it is generally easier to feel drained. This is because you are trying to live life for others. And for her I was just giving her advice that she probably did not want to hear. Once again, because I am part of her family, I saw this as my duty. Shortly after, I started to anticipate when she was going to start talking to me about her problems; these are vices that we can acquire. Once I realized this was happening, I would guide the conversation towards something of common interest, for example: the weather, our children, or other positive situations. This always would work!

Train yourself to get out of situations that affect or drain you. If you could see feelings in colors, you would realize when some place, situation, or person really gets to you. Your mood balances and starts to change. You can clearly feel when there is no balance and then the experience turns into something negative. Do not let this happen. Be aware of the situation, remember that you require to be in balance to achieve your goals and don't ever forget to call on God for spiritual strength.

Learn to mentally observe the mood of the people that surrounds you, and not absorb it emotionally.

For example:

- When you are being defensive in a meeting or with your partner
- When you are around a person who drains your energy and you feel exhausted
- When you are around people with too much energy

If you find yourself in these situations and are consciously attracting them to you, you will be able to respond appropriately.

Staying Grounded

Staying grounded is an easy technique that will help you be calm and remove the excess energy that you have accumulated, which will allow you to avoid an emotional explosion. For example:

- Get in contact with nature. Place your feet or hands on the earth or on the grass. Put your hands, your body, or your feet in direct contact with nature: on a plant, on flowers, or on some other element of nature. Do this very carefully so you do not cause damage. Connecting with nature is a way of healing and you will feel better.
- Clean your office, your car, and your closet. Do some activity that forces you to organize something that is yours or your children's. Center yourself in what you are doing, have fun and enjoy the process.
- If you are a good cook or just love being in the kitchen, cooking will support you at getting grounded as well.
- Paint, dance, draw, or play with your children.
- Exercise. Taking a walk will help change your energy and naturally removes the excess energy you have accumulated.
- If you have no means to do any of the above because you are in your office or some other place inaccessible to nature, turn on relaxation music or natural sounds. Close your eyes for a few minutes and imagine yourself in contact with nature. Let go of negative thoughts by breathing slowly and consciously, and remember you are precious part of this universe and God is reconnecting with you now.

Our Emotions need Respect and Honor

Many people get confused when thinking about Balance. It is believed that thinking positively will eliminate our negative thoughts completely. Thoughts are energy that must go somewhere. They do not disappear because you want them to.

It is important to remember that the first step in any healing process is to understand, recognize, and accept that what has been happening has a reason, you probably don't understand it yet, but it has a purpose. We do not heal anything by blocking it out or pretending it does not exist.

We can make these changes by accepting that there is something bothering us. Then you will realize that other perspectives and ideas do actually exist and expand your possibilities. This helps me so much to ask myself "for what and know why", then I can find a positive approach instead of just judging negatively the situation. This process takes time. Finding Balance is a matter of practice, and you can make a long-term commitment by incorporating consistency with these practices in your daily life.

Learning new ideas, fresh perspectives, and different philosophies are necessary. Gradually let go of old ideas that limit you, and retain those that still work.

I used to believe there was not much I could do with my life circumstances, and that I had no power to change them. When I started adopting the solutions and bringing positive thoughts to my mind in spite of my circumstances, I saw a huge difference in my life.

To create healing and maintain being in the flow, are both processes that take time. Making the decision to do so, and allowing it to be part of lifes practice may seem like a long-term compromise. We are afraid to face our old fears because we feel overwhelmed by them. We should ask ourselves: "What good comes from focusing on matters that have not been emotionally resolved and then result in uncomfortable feelings?" In fact, allowing the healing will free us from carrying this burden of discomfort for the rest of our lives. We have learned to hide from and deny our real feelings in the deeper parts of us, so we then end up showing the world only the parts of us that appear safe.

In our childhood we absorbed many emotional messages. While many of us have learned to repress our feelings, some of us have the opposite problem; where we are easily overwhelmed and emotionally sensitive, which makes us have a hard time maintaining any kind of balance.

For example, anger can be a way to show protection. It can also be a way of recovering your power. However, anger usually comes out in a harmful way for one of two reasons:

- It has been repressed for a long time and then in an instance it can become violent and explosive.
- Someone who tends to act out with anger, is trying to hide and conceal their deep feelings of fear, sadness or guilt

To feel real strength we must accept our weakness. To feel truly powerful we have to allow ourselves to become vulnerable. To experience deep joy we must acknowledge our sadness.

A first step to healing emotionally is knowing the difference between what we think and how we feel. I've noticed that if someone asks: How do you feel about this? We do not answer: "I think that I am good ."

Recognize the difference. What goes through your head is what you think. What goes through your heart is how you feel.

Reconnect Through Nature

Animals

Animals have incredible presence and are beautifully adaptive. Each of their characteristics is unique to how they exist in nature. This representation lends for a perfect lesson of how we ourselves can be our essence in any given situation.

Plants & Trees

Another magnificent representation in nature is plants and trees. The sweet inspiration of sweetness from flowers, strength of benevolent trees, and the endless balancing facets of the plant kingdom in our natural environment. Just by sitting under a tree or walking in the woods you can feel their presence.

Breathing is an Important Practice

To live and love your spirit, breathing is essential. In fact, your respiration is part of your spirit. The air you take in gives you life. Breathing deeply is calling your soul to take air into every cell of your body.

One of the first things that will happen when you are released and detangled from the confusion of a false ego is that you start retaining breath. When your body does not get enough oxygen, it sinks deep in fear and anxiety. That creates a vicious cycle of negativity. Breathing is an essential task in order to be connected. There are many ways to do it.

Nostril Breathing

Practice this exercise: Breathe through alternating nostrils.

Breathing through the left nostril will help calm you. Breathing through the right nostril has an energizing effect. Sit in a simple position. Keep your back straight and relax your shoulders. Count to eight with each inhalation and exhalation.

With your right thumb close the right nostril. Keep the rest of the fingers pointing to the sky.

Inhale through the left nostril. Using the same hand, with your pinky finger close the left nostril, then exhale the breath through the right nostril.

Inhale through the right nostril (always inhale through the nostril you have just used to exhale). Close it with your thumb. Exhale through the left nostril. Inhale through the left nostril and continue for a minimum of 2 to 3 minutes. Repeat the exercise, starting with the left side.

Some benefits:

- You balance both hemispheres of the brain.
- You calm down.
- Your mental state becomes neutralized.
- Your nerves are calmed, which can be especially useful before a difficult conversation.
- Daily practice helps to relieve anxiety.

UNDERSTANDING YOUR BODY

"Medicine lies inside you but you do not use it.
Disease comes from you but you do not notice it."

Hansrat Ali, Free Writer.

One of the quickest ways of tuning in and feeling Balanced is by listening to and understanding the feedback that our physical body gives us. Our Balance is guided by intuition, and intuition talks through the physical body and the heart. If it spoke to us through the mind, our ego would not allow intuition to be real, and we would end up thinking that what we heard or received was fantasy.

Remember that your body is part of a whole. It is the instrument, the vehicle, through which we fulfill our lives. When experiencing physical pain like a headache or backache, fatigue, or any other sickness, your body is trying to send you a sign. The intensity or strength of that signal parallels with the importance of the message that your body wants to give you. Your body is a perfect channel. If you are making the right decisions aligned with the purpose of your life and are balanced, you will feel healthy, calm, and relaxed. You will also have a lot of energy.

In addition, you will be free from pains, anxiety, and stress. However, if you are making bad decisions or are going against the flow, your body will let you know in one way or another. If you understand the signs and make the necessary adjustments to restore Balance, your body will relax and return to a healthy state. If you let your ego speak and ignore the signs your body is giving you for a long time, your body will turn up the volume of the message it is trying to send you, and it will keep trying until you end up sick.

The famous author, Louise L. Hay[1], teaches us how to read the signs, and through positive phrases of her book, *Heal Your Body*, she teaches us how to transform illness.

---

[1] Louise L. Hay, international author, is recognized for her self-help books, between which excels self-healing and the power of affirmations.

Respect & Love Your Body

Our appearance makes us feel good, and it is important that we keep in mind that we should not be looking to improve our body to receive approval from others. What defines pretty and ugly is too subjective, and nowadays that seems to be determined by whatever is in the media.

During my childhood, most girls wanted to look like those blonde, very skinny dolls that were fashionable. To us, they were the ideal and perfect state of beauty. The obsession with weight was uncontrollable.

If we followed the trends, suddenly it was cool to have straight hair, after that curly or dyed... This is all right as long as one knows how to stay within their personal limitations. We must be careful that altering your appearance doesn't lead you to disconnect from yourself and who you really are.

Not long ago, I had a conference with the actual Dalai Lama in Los Angeles, where he reminded us that exterior beauty is only subjective and temporary, and what we really have to cultivate is inner beauty.

This great master told a story of one of his disciples who was recently married. The Dalai Lama wanted to prove his confidence and so he told him, "You have married and I congratulate you, yet I want to tell you that your wife is not pretty, she's quite ugly!" And the alumni answered, "Your sanctity, you taught us that inner beauty is more important than external beauty, and my wife is extremely beautiful inside."

It is very important to nurture and love one's physical body but without forgetting our inner selves. Use your body as if it were your best friend. Do not abuse it. Do not try to saturate it. Remember it is your vehicle and it allows you to serve your spirit and for you to fulfill the purpose of your life.

When you stand in front of a mirror, remember to see yourself with the eyes of your soul. Look at the child inside of you. Do not criticize yourself. To love yourself is to love your body. Talk to it softly. Remember that if you want to ride in this vehicle, your sports car, you need to change the oil, wash the windows, and give it some gas; otherwise, you will not get anywhere.

The tendency we have of speaking to ourselves negatively is so deeply engrained in us that we are not aware of it. When we listen to people speaking about their bodies, a commonly heard word is "hate." "I hate my hair, my nails, my teeth, my wrinkles," and so on. Would you say this to a loved one, or to a friend? Of course you wouldn't. Right?

Let's begin from the inside out in the following example:

Louise L. Hay, one of my favorite writers, teaches in her book, *You Can Heal Your Life*, positive sentences we should repeat according to our sickness.

One of my favorite positive statements, that I said to myself in the mirror every day when I was looking for Balance in my life, is this one:

"I love myself, I honor myself, I deserve the best!"

Remember to talk to your body and to yourself positively. Here are some suggestions:

- You, body, you are so reliable. Thanks for waking me up and taking me through each day.
- You are intelligent, creative, and fun. I know I can count on you.
- You are healthy, strong, and powerful. I appreciate all the things you do for me.

You can also speak in the same way to your spirit:

- I am glad you are here.
- I love you.

Start with the basics. Every human body needs large amounts of water, grains, and proteins. Eat more organic food, especially vegetables and fruit, and eat less canned and fried food.

Then, move a little bit. Movement makes the body happy, and a happy body helps to feed the joy of the spirit. Stand up, do not be lazy, stretch, walk or wiggle 30 minutes per day and three times a week. This keeps the engine of the heart, lungs, and digestive system working.

Have a balanced diet. Eat a healthy breakfast. Try different fruits. Eat an array of colors. Enjoy every meal of every day. Take your time when you eat. Always remember that you deserve your experiences, eating included.

When taken care of and loved, your body becomes the best system of intuitive feedback. It can warn you of danger with a premonition, by sending goose bumps down the back of your neck or giving you chills all the way up and down your arms. It can express excitement through the sensation of heat on your throat or butterflies in your stomach. It can also provide some sense of relief in your heart.

Healing your Physical Body

Healing your body and taking care of it daily means being healthy, satisfied, and in good shape. The three main reasons for which we must keep our body healthy are:

- To survive and keep our wishes and physical needs satisfied.
- To allow us to perceive inner sensations and the external world.
- To maintain a healthy and Balanced relationship with our planet and nature.

In this culture our lifestyle is becoming more and more sedentary and unnatural. More people are living in the cities, with little to no access to nature. While we drive for long hours, walking is an unusual activity. We work in air conditioned buildings with no natural light or fresh air. We eat processed foods. Our lives are full of stress. We steal from our body its natural energy, and we feel drained. We, therefore, consume caffeine to keep up and keep on living in our artificial system of life.

Today's society emphasizes technology and intellectual development. As a result, we are becoming more disconnected from our feelings and needs. If we evaluate part of the scientific tradition, it focuses on external causes and cures of diseases, but it ignores internal causes and the process of healing that the body is asking for. We see ourselves as victims of diseases that, unfortunately, touch us in "X" point of our lives and seemingly with no particular reason.

My dad was in intensive care at the beginning of 2009 for a month and a half suffering from a very serious disease for his age. He had severe pancreatitis, hospital pneumonia, and was very close to needing a tracheotomy. He stayed in intensive care for over a month. This situation was very difficult for our family, especially for my mother. She suffered a lot. Every day doctors kept giving us less encouraging news. We prayed together during the entire month every day. Always our focus was my dad's recovery and his wellness. When we had lost almost all hope, we received a phone call to tell us my dad had been able to remove the oxygen device and did not need a tracheotomy anymore. The lesson for each of us, including my mom, my sisters, and me, was huge. We learned to forgive, work as a team, and listen to our bodies. Each and every one of the signals that our bodies gave us were lessons that meant we needed to stop and listen. If we did not listen and pay attention, the alarm would get louder, more severe, and often unrepairable. Today my dad, at almost 80 years old, is happy and calm in the caring hands of my mother.

The condition of our health often depends on medicine, for which I have an infinite amount of respect and admiration, but the responsibility to our health, is also ours. The emphasis on external cures has led our modern society to turn into a drug-oriented culture. Most of the time it seems that we are looking for a "magic pill" to relieve us. We all know that these days drugs, alcohol, cigarettes, food, and other addictions make us hide our real emotional state as well as "drown" the signals of our physical body.

Our body needs to get sick and send signals to catch our attention. Fortunately society is starting to awaken as we begin to see the importance of balanced nutrition and regular exercise. Lots of people are taking responsibility for their health by creating and maintaining their own physical health and wellness plans.

The healing begins when we synchronize with our body, meaning we feel it and hear it. The human body knows what it needs. It communicates with us very clearly and specifically if we are willing to hear it. We must cultivate the art of understanding it and listen to the signals it emits. Our body constantly tells us if we are giving it the right food, or if it is the right hour to do something -- to rest, to sleep, or to move.

To hear our body's signals and to understand them, we first must detox our whole body, hear it, and love it. Realize that your body works 24 hours a day, 7 days a week to keep you as alive and as healthy as possible. Put into practice loving your body. When you see yourself in front of a mirror, do not criticize. Your body is not asking for big things. For example, taste your food; the more natural the better, and if you have children teach them how to do this, too. Watch the sunset, smell the flowers, listen to relaxing music, get a massage.

There is one way that I have learned to heal the body, which is by considering animals. They eat when they are hungry and rest when they are tired; in doing so, they naturally replenish their energy and vitality. Of course, our lives are more complex and we cannot be as spontaneous as animals because of all of our commitments, but we can cultivate the habit of checking in with our body every day. It will not take more than 15 minutes to do this.

Remember, it is in this life, in our physical body, that the levels of our existence lie and are shown. Our physical body expresses if we are unbalanced in the spiritual, mental, or emotional aspect of ourselves. Of course, it shows imbalance in a physical way if we have not heard it otherwise.

For example, if we are under pressure in our job, so that our emotional and spiritual needs are not being given consideration, we can be sure that our physical body is going to force us to slow down and get back to our emotional and spiritual needs.

Any disease or accident is a clear marker of the need to look deeply into our being, our interior, and our lives, and to make changes.

My Body asked for a Break and I Ignored It

A couple of months ago I had been traveling for a long period with a considerable amount of work. I had interviews, I often had ten consultations a day -- all of them classified as "urgent," and I did several workshops without a break. My journey lasted a little over a month. My husband could not go with me, and I had two young children back home. The pressure of being a mom and not having them by my side was hard. The help of my family, especially my sister, was invaluable. The journey back to California was quite long. I spent almost 23 hours in airports, at customs, and traveling. For weeks, my body kept asking me to rest, and I did not hear it because "I did not have time." The result of this was that, when I got home, two cysts showed up on my right ovary, one of which was nine centimeters in diameter. Could I have avoided this? Maybe yes, but "time" was in the way. So I went to the doctor and was given two choices: either endure the pain and wait for the cyst to disappear or surgery. I tried to understand what was happening to me before making a decision. I cannot deny that I was scared because the pain was difficult to bear and occurring with greater frequency every day. Two friends and my husband took me for treatment, and I was finally able to understand the holistic meaning of the myoma: "let go of the past, understand the lessons it gave me, and look ahead."

I was so thankful to my body for sending me this signal through the cyst, and I got the message. Physical pain was part of my spiritual growth and, of course, part of my awakening. My body was desperately asking for a pause, rest, and for me to meditate.

To know how to say no, I established priorities. I learned to go back to my routine and do what I like most.

After three weeks I had a second ultrasound, and the cyst was gone! The pain stopped in two and a half weeks, and I felt an evolution in the process of awakening. I thank the cyst for showing up and teaching me a lesson. Thanks to this experience, I have learned to love and honor my physical body more.

To hear your body requires practice and patience. Cultivate this ability, write what you feel when it talks. Maybe at the beginning it will be silent. Do not worry if you do not understand; do not feel guilty or judge yourself for being sick. Having a good diet, drinking water, exercising, thinking positively, and visualizing are sometimes not enough to avoid getting sick. Life is complex, and sometimes mysterious. Our inner voice uses any resources it has to teach us.

If we allow ourselves to learn through our sicknesses, to grow and go deeper into our existence and into our wisdom, we can see disease as a gift as well as an opportunity for change and growth.

When it comes to pain, fear, and confusion created by disease, we must keep the door open to be guided by our inner light, our inner guide, and our intuition. We must always ask ourselves: What do I need to learn from this sickness? And remember to keep our hearts open to receive the message.

Meditation to Connect with your Body

This meditation will teach you how to communicate with your physical body. Read it first and then practice it.

Start in a relaxing position. You can be seated or lying down, with your eyes closed. Relax and be as far away from noise as possible.

As you relax you will realize that your thoughts do not stop going through your mind. Intentionally remove them from your mind, let them go consciously. Every time one of them shows up, let it go. When you see the next one, let it go as well.

An easy way to let thoughts go is as follows: Every time a thought comes up, count ONE, TWO and breathe slowly and deeply. Every time you exhale, think of focus and calm. THREE, FOUR... slowly.

Now imagine that you are in a place surrounded by nature, where no one can bother or interrupt you. It is a magical place that belongs to you.

Allow your conscience to scan your body, starting from your feet. Contract your fingers and hold them like that for a couple of seconds. Relax. Let them perceive the place where you are.

Now, contract your face, hold it, and rest. Do this exercise with your neck, head, shoulders, legs, pelvis, hips, abdomen, arms, hands, and back. Notice your thoughts; count them if you can, and then let them go consciously.

Now allow your mind to follow your breathing. Try to breathe with the sound of the waves. Every time you inhale, feel how the air fills your lungs. When you exhale, let your lungs rest.

Let your conscience move through your body and touch every part that needs attention. It does not matter the reason for the attention -- perhaps it is even pain that brings your conscience to that part of your body. Your body will ask for this attention because something is not working properly or it is tired. Maybe one part of your body is not feeling accepted by you or by others.

Put your hands on the area you are focusing on and pay attention to this part of your body. Ask it how it feels, what it needs, or what it wants to tell you. Listen, visualize, or imagine what it is feeling.

Imagine your body talking. What is it telling you?

Realize what is happening with your hands and around your body.

Now, if you feel it, I want you to imagine love, healing energy, from the source. Allow it to enter your body, each and every cell, through your hands, and to every part that needs to be cured.

Imagine a beautiful light, warm, maybe gold or whatever color your body needs. Send acceptance, love, and healing to that part of your body.

Imagine that healing energy dissolving your pain, tension, sickness, or lack of love. Imagine it sending fresh energy and vitality to your body.

Now look with your inner eyes at your healthy, beautiful, and energetic body.

When you feel ready, remove your hands from your body, stretch a little bit, take a deep breath, open your eyes, and write down your experience if you want to.

LEARN TO VISUALIZE

How does a six-year-old child visualize?
"Make a wish, imagine it coming true,
add some colors, smile and feel the joy."

Jasmine, Tara Redwood Preschool, California

What is Visualization?

Visualization is imagining whatever we would like to achieve. It is daydreaming: imagining yourself in a place you would like to be, for example, the sea or the mountains.

When you mentally anticipate a situation, you are visualizing. When you are about to begin a big project or simply make dinner, you can imagine it before It actually happens.

Visualization means having an image, an idea, of what you want to create. To achieve your goals (no matter what they are) one of the main steps is visualization. Imagine your reality becoming what you want. A great American tennis player, Andre Agassi, confessed recently that before every match he used to imagine and visualize his plays, and then during the game he did them.

Another great step is to imagine how you would feel once you have achieved your goal. Now, bring this feeling into your present reality and create this way of being as if you have already achieved your goal; this is the key!

Turning our negative thoughts into positive ones can change our awareness inwardly and outwardly in our environment.

Not often do human beings exploit the full potential of their minds. Many believe that success means to be rich or have the material things we desire. Success is really to live a full, meaningful, healthy, and happy life, knowing that we are not defined by the situations that happen to us, but by the way we respond to them. Every step of our life is an opportunity to learn, to evolve, and to improve our material environment.

There are many people who get used to thinking in a negative way. It becomes normal for them to keep thinking like that for the rest of their lives, with a feeling of resignation, as if there is no other way to perceive life. Despite their habitual negative thoughts, the fact is that nobody wants to create disease, poverty, anguish, or discontent.

The brain does not sleep when the rest of our bodies do. It keeps working for or against us. That is why we must learn to control it. It is like training a puppy to do what you ask him to do, but that also requires correction, discipline, and consistency.

Ask yourself everyday: What makes me happy?

If we visualize health, prosperity, energy, or happiness, that is what we will get. We will create our future reality. It is a privilege we have had since we were born. Remember we can visualize our deepest wishes for our lives.

Everything in around us is a subject designed by an idea. Change is a process; it does not happen from night to day; it is a job you must perform which you will surely be able to accomplish. However, if you stop for a second to think, you will realize that this ability has been given to us unconsciously. It is as though we are watching the world through a pair of glasses that we do not even know we wear every day.

We believe that the world is what we see through those glasses, or what has been recorded in a file. But if we see that our environment has created a perception for us, or society has created it, and we take those glasses off for a second, we start to see our life in a different way. We stop being victims and start to understand the process of creation. From this point on, we will be able to understand in a better way our system of beliefs and to consciously choose our ideas, attitudes, and expectations.

Writing our beliefs and repetitive thoughts helps us bring them to our conscience, acknowledge which of those are helping us grow spiritually, and which of them limit us or interfere with creating what we really want to do in our lives. When we are aware of our beliefs, those that we need to dissolve will start to disappear, and those that really support the purpose of our life will start to grow.

Visualize What You Really Want

When we learn to identify what we like to do, when we remember the essence of what we enjoyed doing when we were children, we reconnect with our inner child. In turn, our energy increases, making us vibrate and flow easily. This allows our inner being to express itself. In turn, we will be able to change rigid patterns we might have in our brain.

What are the things that you connect with so thoroughly that you lose all sense of time and space and simply enjoy the moment? The answer to that question will say a lot about you. Take a moment and write down your answer. Make a quick list of all the things you love and you will see how your inner voice will try to be heard. If you are connected with you inner child, you will be able to express yourself better, and you will get to know truly what it is you want to do.

When I wrote my answers, I remembered how much I like:

- Dancing with my sister and singing together after school.
- Walking barefoot on the sand, watching the sea.
- Talking to the plants in the backyard of my house, sometimes even watering them, and enjoying what they give me.
- Feeling the energy of a tree that is in a park near my house. I used to find it fascinating to sit behind it and make wishes.

- Helping poor children, making them feel good with a smile, playing with them, or bringing them food and clothes.
- Feeling free and uncontrolled.

I remember when I was a child I used to love being the monitor of my class and arranging the bulletin boards. I also remember my mom used to get upset about this because every day I brought her "a new project." I also remember that I used to love playing with my teacher.

Let's do an exercise:

Write down here what you like to do the most and the things that make your heart vibrate:

The less you think, the faster you write, the better. Write all the things you love. Do not spend over five minutes on this.

Study your list; this will help you bond with your spirit, temperament, and energy.

Some ideas?

- Explore nature
- Read
- Make up stories
- Play with animals
- Make up games
- Study how things work
- Sports
- Music

- _____
- _____
- _____
- _____
- _____
- _____
- _____
- _____
- _____
- _____

When you are finished, consider how this exercise went for you. If the outcome is not positive, begin by reaffirming your skills right now! Your natural gifts and your unique intelligence can be found in those activities and interests. Get back in touch with your passions, with your gifts. If you need to heal them, look for ways to start developing those interests. For example, you could read more about those people you admire the most.

If working with people is your passion, enroll as a volunteer in a social organization. When I arrived in California I worked as a volunteer. There I learned about the system, and at the same time I looked for a job through the workshops they offered. My volunteering was doing administrative activities 10 hours a week. It was a spectacular experience.

I met a lot of people, older people, from whom I learned respect and compassion. I had the amazing opportunity to speak in public for the first time because part of the volunteer project was to make a 5-minute presentation for 25 people. I did a presentation about the country of Colombia, where I am from. I taught the audience about my people, Colombian coffee, and Columbia's landscapes... While preparing my presentation, it seemed to me that those 5 minutes would be an eternity, but they were not! Do you know why? Because I was talking about something I feel passionate about, Colombia, and I was learning how to do something new.

Nowadays I still work for this organization, giving seminars to help people gain security in themselves. Also, we help people look for a job after figuring out what they really want to do, instead of merely doing something they thought they should be doing.

Thinking Clearly

Our inner wisdom can help us accomplish what we want, as long as we are clear and specific with our thoughts.

When I begin working with my clients, I always ask about the goals that each person wants to achieve in every level of their lives. As time passes, we reach a point where the person can see more clearly what they want, they have unloaded their baggage, and it is easier for them to have inner clarity, wisdom and tranquility. Realization & ability to know what they want to create.

Having clear and transparent intentions means that you will not accept anything different from what you wish for, or from what you deserve. If you are not sure of what you want, imagine yourself in the best scenario possible, and remember to enjoy the ride, don't wait until the end to enjoy the process. Every single day that you ask for your desires, it will turn up different. Some will be mundane and others will be amazing.

Remember to always ask in the present and give thanks. From the first book of Neale Donald Wash[2], *Conversations with God,* one sentence he asks his readers to write down or repeat daily is: "Thank God for the success I have achieved." The first time I read this sentence I asked myself a couple of times: "Achieved success? Hmmmmm, which one?" I shared it with my husband and he wrote the sentence in his journal and we began to read it every day at the same time, by his suggestion. In the beginning it sounded rather weird to me, but later I started to feel the success being a part of me. I started to understand that part of the achieved success is the air I breathe every day, the water I drink, the sunset I watch from my office, my children, my husband, my family, my friends, and the city I live in. These are all part of the success in my life.

Making the Map of My Dreams

A couple of years ago while meditating, feeling calm, clear, and relieved from my emotions which used to be a rollercoaster, I felt in my heart the words: "map of prosperity." Beyond the three resolutions from New Year's Eve, I had never written down what I wanted or wished for before now. And then, I wrote my deepest wishes for the next year. One month later, I placed my wishes, with the artistic help of my husband, on a poster that I would like to share with you.

---

[2]   Neale Donald Walsh, world reknown author of the trilogy, *Conversations with God - Talking with God,* shows in his book a new way to relate to the Creator.

Now I Invite You to Make Yours!

One day, when you are alone, and even better if you are outside in nature and very calm, gather: one poster board, markers, magazines, paints, pictures of your family, and a pen and paper.

Then, take a few minutes to breathe deeply and begin to feel what you really want. Remember, you have unloaded your bags and you do not need anything else; you are ready to express your destiny.

Observe nature.

Pick a relaxing music CD, natural sounds, or some other sound that inspires you.

Divide the poster into five parts: spiritual, professional, health, prosperity, and family. It does not matter if the sections are the same size. Leave fear aside; surround yourself with love and tranquility. Allow your inner voice to talk through this poster board. Paste pictures. For example, if your dream is to travel to Greece, then include a picture of the Parthenon. Or if you want your family to be healthy, include a picture of them or someone who represents them, and write the word health.

**The more specific and creative you are,
the better your creation will be!**

When you feel that you have fully expressed your vision with pictures and words, color your masterpiece as if you were a child. Draw lines, hearts, whatever you want.

Finally, give thanks and admire your masterpiece. It contains wishes placed from the bottom of your heart.

Do not forget to laminate it or, if you want, frame it. Put it somewhere where you can see it during the next 21 days, and hopefully even longer.

The Power of Words

Words have an absolutely powerful energy. When we say them we can create conditions and circumstances in our lives, as if words were a magic wand. Each word has a particular intonation and frequency that vibrates with the intention of attracting.

Words have the power to destroy or create what you wish for. If you want to have a better lifestyle, each word you say must be said with a tone of love, in harmony, and with lots of peace. Let your words be guided by your inner voice.

My client Jennifer, began her session by saying she did not know how she wanted to continue her professional career. She mentioned several times that she just wanted to go home. Prior to our meeting, she thought she was surrounded by people who did not accept and support her.

We had six sessions of constant work to open her heart and form trust. She experienced a beautiful process of re-connecting, unblocking, and forgiving herself and everyone else, including her bosses and co-workers. Jennifer was surprised because after eight months her boss proposed to transfer her to her country, which was a goal that she set in her Prosperity Map. Upon completion of our work together, she was so happy with her job, she did not even want to go back home any longer.

Opening our heart when it comes to what we say, feel, and how we say it is very important because our inner source listens and understands the intentions that we emit. God understood Jennifer's message and heard it. The power of words is so strong!

Words must be clear enough to create and express what we want; our heart must be fully open.

My friend Luciano was going to a psychologist because he was having communication problems in his marriage. The counselor's advice was to tell the truth to his wife and communicate openly with her. He then talked to his wife and told her everything he had kept been keeping inside, which, for many reasons, hurt her self-esteem. The result was that his wife, with her heart completely broken, lost security in herself. Of course, without even understanding what was going on, she reacted aggressively, and a couple months later they divorced.

Telling the truth is generally the right thing to do, but perhaps not to the extent that it hurts someone else's feelings. When we tell the truth from our heart we must try to understand what the other person is trying to teach us. Then, communication becomes an art and a discipline that gets in touch with our heart, builds confidence and heals.

Ask yourself how you must communicate your wishes. If you really want to change an important thing in your life, remember that words are like bricks. If you allow negative words to come out of you, you cannot expect to build a huge monument of your life.

Watch and Listen Carefully to What Surrounds You

Learning how to speak is important. It is also important to surround yourself with words and positive messages.

My friend Chris completed her Prosperity Map and achieved every goal she intended to reach through our training. She felt happy because after eight sessions she managed to end a stormy relationship of three years, change her tedious job for another that filled her with joy and met her expectations, and, most importantly, she was able to feel calm again.

Nevertheless, at her new job she was feeling awkward with her co-workers. Her sensitivity level was quite high and was experiencing tension in her work environment. In one of our sessions I asked her about her colleagues because, truth be told, I could not understand how she could still feel so dissatisfied while having the job of her dreams. She told me about her two best friends at work who talk every day with her bosses. Her friends were aware of how everyone dressed, who was going to be fired first, what he or she said, etc. Of course, Chris ended up involved in this gossipy situation and it was affecting her very negatively.

It is not about not accepting reality, but if someone makes you feel uncomfortable or is not providing something positive for your life, you must simply walk away. If, suddenly, the person sitting next to you starts to gossip, change the subject to something more interesting. If the gossiping continues, simply tell them that if our conversation is not positive, then you prefer to not be a part of it.

It is not necessary to criticize others or reject them. In a calm and positive way you can set an example and explain to them the power of words in your life. The best way to fully aware is to make every thought and every word you say or hear positive and calm.

I remember a company I once worked for made it a priority to keep their personnel highly motivated. To achieve this they organized motivational conferences and speakers to visit. At one such conference, the host told us that when people asked him how he was doing, he always answered, "Incredible, but getting better." Unusual, right? It is really interesting to answer like this instead of saying, "Hmmmm, I'm okay..." Try responding with, "I am INCREDIBLY FINE! Thank you..."

Once I took my children to their gymnastics class, and because it was raining I let them stay for an additional hour of lessons. I stayed home for a while waiting for the rain to stop. During this time I listened to the conversation two friends were having.

"It has been raining so much; we are going to have rain for two days in a row."

"This is fantastic," answered the friend. "Can you imagine? We will have more harvest and the environment is cleaning up. It's about time it starts raining..."

"Yes," said the other one, "I'll put my children in their boots and a coat and we'll enjoy the day."

Frankly, I was shocked with the conversation. On the way home with my children I got a phone call from a relative back in Colombia, and he said: "What a bummer, it never stops raining in this city. The rain makes it so boring here, I am just fed up with rain!"

It is complicated to live in a big city while it is raining, that I know. However, it is also important to appreciate what is going on around us and show gratitude. If we do not, we may miss the opportunity to appreciate many things.

Practice communicating in a positive way every day. Remember, you must be disciplined about the way you talk to yourself, how you express your wishes, what you are hearing from everybody else, and even how you express appreciation for what surrounds you.

Watch how the environment around you starts to change. You will feel calmer. Your heart will start to open and your life will turn into something very special.

Expand your vocabulary, avoid words like "I hate," "stupid," "I die for," "I am fed up with." Replace them with positive words that inspire you. See every situation as an opportunity to improve. Do this short exercise when you talk about something that happened to you in your day: Talk about it in a negative way, and then again in a positive way. How does this exercise make you feel?

Check Your Thoughts

Controlling your thoughts is essential, and this is something that really worries my clients after making their Prosperity Map. Knowing how important daily Balance is for bringing consciousness to our thoughts, they tell me that what worries them is what their thoughts are saying or what they think is going to happen.

You must be aware of your thoughts. If they frighten you, it may be because you can feel the results of your inner voice. If your thoughts are not in agreement with your inner voice, it is logical that your inner voice will not follow you in this kind of thought. Whenever you feel nervous, you must understand that your inner voice is giving you an alarm to let you know that you are going against the flow, and that your thoughts are not helping you.

However, this does not mean that something bad will happen to you. If you catch your thoughts in time you can change them. To understand this, you can remember when you were a child driving a car in a video game, always aware of not crashing into other cars. When an oncoming car or an obstacle approached, you would avoid it and then keep on going.

It is all a matter of practice. Let go of the oars and sail through the river of life with the help of your compass (your heart). Release your fears, direct yourself, and soon you will arrive at your goal.

When you feel good and flow toward the things you wish for, the people surrounding you -- your children, your partner, your co-workers -- will be affected by your example, and you will see how they ask about your change.

Marcelo, my client, is the director of a technology company in Argentina. It was very difficult for him to have good communication with his co-workers, especially his boss. When we began working together he felt calmer, but the changes in his job where incredibly noticeable after "letting go of the oars." He let go of his fears, to them focus on what he wanted. He pushed away all the negativity, and several days later he told me his boss asked him about how his life changed; all of his co-workers started to ask him for advice about how to be in Balance at work.

At the beginning, Marcelo justified his fear and thought it was natural and valid. He focused too much on the negative aspects of his coworkers, on his long days of work, and so on. Most people focus almost every thought as an answer to the things that happened to them in life. He used to ask himself: "Why is this happening to me?" And the answer was simple: Everything that happens is a result of our thoughts and repetitive emotions.

After some time, Marcelo finally learned surround himself with positiveness and changed his environment, not only in his work but also with his colleagues, choosing to have positive thoughts and going with the flow. With a little bit of practice he began to watch people in different settings and experience with the eyes of his inner being, fearlessly, and began to enjoy going to work.

Invitations for the Week

Discover your gifts.

Make your Prosperity Map.

Surround yourself with people who are positive.

Regularly meditate to visualize your projects.

Visit *www.theblueleaf.com*, where you will find meditations for various purposes.

TRUST YOUR INTUITION

*Find the sunshine in your interior;
it's time to believe in you!*

**Akira, 6-years-old,
Tara Redwood Preschool, California**

Since we were young we learned how to repress our feelings: "Be brave and sleep alone, the monster does not exist." We did not believe in our feelings and we did not express them clearly, afraid that people might say something. We learned to get comfortable with the situations surrounding us, and we ignored what we wanted to do, just to please others. We also blocked our emotions by pretending they did not exist or just blocking the situations. We learned to do things only because everyone else expected it of us.

Instead of looking for approval from our inner guidance, we looked to authority, and then we let go of our inner power. As time went by, we started feeling like the victim -- anxious and, some of us become depressed and empty.

The reality is that we have to re-educate ourselves to listen and believe our truth, that same truth that comes through our inner voice. Learning to act according to that truth, even when sometimes we believe it is our imagination and that we are going to fail, is essential. We need not always follow the rules or have an external security as a consequence of the approval that surrounds us.

Our mind, our intellect, is a very powerful tool that we have to train to work under the guidance of our inner wisdom or intuition. As we move forward toward change, it is necessary to acknowledge that intuition is a valid source of information and guidance.

What is Intuition?

To many scientists, thinkers, and artists, their intuition is the key to most discoveries.

They describe it as a knack, a gift, susceptible of being cultivated, that in some situations having an immediate knowledge, with no help or reason. We all have the ability to intuit on some level. Philosophers, musicians, artists, and scientists from all times – from Arquimedes to Newton to Einstein -- owe their important discoveries and the inspiration of their best works to intuition. For example, Einstein said, "When it comes to making science, the only valuable thing is intuition." Salvador Dali, when painting, waited for "the time of occurrence of the delusion, through a systematic and wise attitude to the irrational phenomena."

Although it is established that intuitive intelligence is innate in every person, a gift, the question is: Where does the information generated during these perceptions come from? Does it come from inside us? Is it about a divine inspiration, a universal connection?

Reconnect with your being, your inner voice. This is the last level of Balance. This happens naturally when we connect to the other three levels. The more you connect with your inner voice, your source, the less you will be guided by the fearful dialogue of your ego, and you will start to deeply listen to the song of life. You will be able to hear and filter the world's messages.

A few years ago I saw a movie called "Earth", I found it beautiful and very helpful to our daily lives. The movie is about how animals survive and spend thousands of circumstances to rediscover the source of life: WATER.

They survive in adverse circumstances as climate changes and of course the lack of food and water. They travel very long paths without be afraid or go backwards, in other words they PERSIST! If we persist a little more like these animals, which are focused on their paths, then we would achieve ALL our goals, right?

Elephant's herds in Africa walk thousands of miles, avoiding obstacles of the environment, and always working in team. They travel with the certainty that their target is the water. We also seek the REAL SOURCE: Prosperity, Health, Love, our growth. Let us be guided by our heart. Forget the ego, and start using our little guide called intuition. Elephants have no maps, no GPS, they just know how to keep their hearts (instinct) open.

The more you strengthen you relationship with your inner voice, the faster the mental chatter of your ego will shut down. Insecurity will start to disappear and you will find yourself. You will start listening to your inner guide. As a GPS (Global Positioning System) in a car that guides you efficiently from point A to point B, your inner radar will send you right to where your deepest wishes are.

Receive your Intuition

Learning to believe in our intuition is a process, and, furthermore, it may be considered an art. You do not learn from one moment to the next. Once you disconnect your ego, it is important to allow your inner voice to talk.

Of course, your ego will try to mock every new idea by saying, "Who do you think you are? That is ridiculous." Ego is that inner voice we hear all the time saying: "You cannot do this," "You will fail," or "You will not make it."

It is not so hard to distinguish your ego from your intuition. Once you connect with your intuition, you will feel calm and positive, and experience heightened awareness. When you connect with your ego, you will feel criticized and depressed, and will have little awareness. That`s how easy it is to distinguish between your ego and your intuition.

When you first try to connect with your inner self you will hear quite a lot of inner voices: childhood memories, others' opinions, fears, doubts, and, perhaps, good ideas, also.

Maybe the first weeks of practice you will hear your mind contradicting itself. For example, if your intuition says, "Relax, everything is alright," you will hear an inner voice saying, "You cannot do it, you lose."

The truth is that if you follow your intuition you will be able to feel calm, happy, full of energy, and Balanced. On the other hand, when you are listening to your ego, you will feel depressed, absent, and lethargic.

To connect with your intuition, you must observe what you are saying to yourself at least twice a day. The inner voice can use different resources to talk: words, images, feelings, a book, a friend, a teacher, etc.

Tips to Start Listening to your Intuition

Thanking is trusting

As you wake up in the morning, begin your day by giving thanks. It does not matter how you are feeling or what is going on in your life. Pay attention to the fact that you are alive for another day, which is a gift from the Creator. It can be spoken aloud or mentally, however you prefer.

When I was returning home from Brazil I met an optometrist on the airplane. Our flight was delayed 3 hours, so after talking with him for a while, he shared some rather personal things. From the moment he made the following statement, I have tried to practice it and teach my children: "Everyday I give thanks for all the simple and relevant things in this life." For example, while washing his hands, he breathes deeply and says, "Thank God for water, how good it is to feel it." At dawn, he gives thanks for the colors nature allows us to see, etc.

Do this short exercise and write three things you are thankful for:

I am thankful for:

_____

_____

_____

I am thankful for:

_____

_____

_____

I am thankful for:

_____

_____

_____

While you practice focusing on your daily blessings, the list will increase. Repeat this exercise for the next three days.

When you go to a restaurant, you usually order and then relax. Maybe you have a drink while your food is being prepared. Perhaps you enjoy the company of family or friends. But surely you would not follow the waiter to the kitchen to speak with the chef. You trust in being in the right place to receive what you asked for, right? That is how your intention works! Just believe you will get what you ask for. Trust!

Open the Door to Intuition

Every time you are stressed or preoccupied, breathe as I suggested before until you feel relaxed and focused.

Every time you inhale, mentally welcome intuition (God, inner wisdom) into your body. Think that you are inviting someone you love and that he or she will help you. Feel tranquility when this enters your body. Realize how this energy fills your lungs, your heart, your mind, and, finally, your cells. Feel comfortable with this vision.

Imagine it with colors or smells, whatever is easier for you. Do not rush in this exercise; take your time. Ego likes to run through the day creating a false sense of urgency. Imagine ego doing this, while intuition goes inside your body slowly and calmly.

Once you feel focused and calm, place both hands over your emotions power center (your belly button). From this energy center you make choices and drive your life. Imagine the presence of your source expanding from your heart to your belly, full of compassion. Do this continuously, while visualizing your body filling with light.

Next, imagine yourself holding this energy and say out loud: "I focus my intuition on… for example, "being calm," "exercising," or "finishing my project."

Be quiet and allow yourself to feel tranquility from your heart. Focus on one goal each day.

Inner Voice Signals

Every time we have a problem, there is a message. God tries to call our attention through different situations, which might make us feel uncomfortable or might be an opportunity to change our lives. If we pay attention to little signs, we will certainly learn from them. If we do not, the problems will increase until we do get the message and pay attention.

When something bad happens we often say to ourselves: "Why is this happening to me? I do not deserve this. I am giving THE BEST OF ME!" If you can relate, try to see things from a different point of view. Look from the outside, analyze the lesson quietly, and ask God for help out loud. Say: "I know you are trying to tell me something, but I do not get it."

After asking for signals from God, you must let go of your problem and be aware of every signal. This might come in different ways, so do not specify how it must be delivered. It could come from a friend, or maybe something happens unexpectedly right next to you. The message could come immediately or take its time. The truth is that it will come at the right moment.

Martin, another client of mine, one week after his daughter was born, got a call from his boss telling him he was not going to continue in the position he had been working for the last three years. With no reasons, the boss simply told him to finish his holidays and come back to analyze if there might be another position available within the company. At the beginning he felt scared and, of course, had lots of anxiety, because at the time he was in charge of the family finances. Maria, his wife, had quit her job to take care of their two children. After a week, Martin went back to work and spent a couple of months in a job where he did not feel comfortable at all. He felt isolated and unproductive.

Eventually, Martin understood, through his intuition, that this situation was not a door closing, but an opportunity to keep going forward and do what he wanted to do: work 8 hours a day (instead of working at least 15 hours per day as he did before), spend time with his family, and do work that involved challenges and projects (unlike his previous job). Of course, ego and fear were all around him, and many times he had doubts about going on.

While in this situation that seemed unfair, Martin let go of the subject to God and asked for clear signals of what he needed to do. Soon he got a job offer in another state, with a better salary and under the conditions he wanted.

Understanding the Lessons

The most difficult part of understanding what happens to us in a situation that implies suffering is to understand the lessons and messages that come with it.

There is a motto I try to live every day that has helped me understand the mirrors in life. As Jeronimo R. Ocampo[3] says in his article:

---

[3] Jeronimo R Ocampo, Psychotherapist, Logotherapist, transpersonal, social and spiritual psychologist. Founder of the Human Being Research Center "Yerom" that offers alternative healing and motivation techniques in the city of Buenos Aires, Argentina.

Mirrors in Your Life

Although we want, we cannot live isolated, we cannot be hermits. Maybe under some circumstances this is possible, but isolating does not solve the deepest problems the human being has.

Growing in this life starts from a relationship. The biggest mirror we can use to get to know ourselves and to discover ourselves is the relationships we have with other people. It is in these relationships where we discover our fears, our way of seeing life, and we will be able to see what really motivates us.

If you pay attention to all these people that in some way are and have been part of your life, you will realize that each of them have highlighted some aspect of yourself:

Some uncover your fears, others wake up kindness, others drive you mad, others reveal you as a saint, and others make you hate them.

Others awake infinite love … but, with no doubt, all the things they have awoken have not been awoken in them, but in you.

There is nothing on the outside that can be changed, unless you change what's inside of you. You decide what comes out of you, you decide what comes in, and finally it is this change that transforms your life. Those thousands of mirrors are just doing their work, showing you the right path, the path to your liberation.

Do the test, look into those mirrors without judging or rejecting, and listen to your interior and discover that the power is in your hands.

It is possible that circumstances or people will not change, but if you can change the way you approach and deal with the present, you will change the way you see people you have to meet every day.

If you keep being free, you will not depend on anyone, and you will have taken the first step to awakening. When you think things should change in order for you to be happy, when you think others are the cause of your unhappiness, it depends on you to have a different life, it depends on you to look at the mirror and be free to understand what you see.

Maybe there you will find the meaning of the phrase Jesus once said: "The truth will set you free."

Sitting in a quiet place, slowly and deeply take a few breaths and focus your conscience, together with your wisdom, which at the same time are connected to God. This is enough to understand the message. Feel peace and calm. Either out loud or with your inner voice, ask God to help you understand the lesson and the message clearly. Also, allow your intuition to guide you. The answer is the first feeling, maybe an image, scene, or word that comes to your mind. Write it down. What do you feel is the right thing to do? How do you feel?

You will know you are in the right connection if you feel calm and peaceful inside. You might think you are being guided by your inner voice, your angel, God. If, instead of this, you feel that you are draining your energy and you feel exhausted, it is because you are not letting yourself be guided by intuition, that divine guidance.

Remember that this is a process, because you have been gathering data for years: fears, actions, doubts, etc. Do not forget to recognize that you are surely fighting against your inner feelings.

When I decided to change my major from engineering to the spiritual, my parents and my older sister where shocked, so much that they spent a few years suggesting that I do something different, something profitable. For a long time they thought I had completely lost my mind.

I, of course, could not understand why they were criticizing me, or why they could not understand that what I was doing was coming straight from my heart. I was trying, every time I had a problem or discussion with them, to solve it from my point of view. Communicating this way made me happy and I used to think: "Good, I am showing them that my decision is true." But, truth be told, for them it was just an example of how I could affect their lives. I felt really sad for a long time. I doubted myself so many times. One day I sat down to meditate and asked out loud what the meaning of all the things I was feeling inside was. Why were they judging me? I thought: "Believe in yourself, keep strong when opinions or situations are difficult to bear, keep your serenity. It does not matter what they say about you, if your heart feels happy then believe in your heart. Believe in you and the mirrors will disappear magically." With this experience I began to heal my inner fears.

I took from the book *Living in the Light* by Shakty Gawain[4] the following phrases, which helped me understand the lessons others show us:

Remember:

If you judge and criticize, others will judge and criticize you as well.
If you hurt others, others will do the same to you.
If you lie, others will lie to you, too.
If you are irresponsible with yourself, others will be irresponsible in their relationships with you.

---

[4]   Shakti Gawain is one of the pioneers in personal development. Her books cover topics from manifestation to physical and spiritual sanctions, to richness and prosperity generation.

If you talk trash of yourself, others will talk trash of you.
If you do not listen to your feelings, others will not do it either.
If you love yourself, others will love you, too.
If you believe in yourself, others will believe in you as well.
If you are honest with yourself, others will be honest with you.
If you honor your life, others will honor you.
If you enjoy life, others will enjoy being with you.

Change Takes Time

Remember to change your same old records, the habits of listening to your ego; it is just a matter of time.

Remember to ask for strength from God, release the old and be focus on the new.

The mirrors you create around you are not exclusively negative. You have also created positive things and it is important to concentrate on the positive. Think about the people who love you, the animals, or maybe the love you feel for nature, which you did not even realize you felt before. All of those things, you have created, and they are mirrors, too.

Let Yourself Go With the Flow

Follow the flow, and keep yourself open to feel and hear your heart when it sends you signals. About this, I can give you a clear example of something that happened to me. A couple of years ago the lease from our house was about to expire. We had a big and beautiful house but I did not feel comfortable there; it was too dark. When I suggested to my husband that we move, we realized our budget would not suffice for what we were looking for. After thinking about it, the conclusion we reached was that we had to extend our lease for one more year.

My intuition, however, suggested that we look for other options and stay neutral, although it seemed that all the houses on the market were out of our budget.

I imagined a house filled with light, windows all around, my office in a remote space in the home, and each of my children in their own room.

The day I went to deliver the letter to extend the lease for one more year, the office was closed, so I would have to return to deliver the letter in an hour. I was away from home and did not know what to do during this hour. Suddenly, my intuition asked me to turn on the car and go to the beach, turn right, then after two miles turn left and stop. I was in an unfamiliar place in front of a real estate agency.

I stopped there, asked for a list of houses to rent, and, no surprise, all the houses were extremely expensive. I was disappointed, I cannot deny it, because some of the houses had all the things I was looking for in a house. I went to check out one of the houses that caught my attention.

I arrived at the house and loved it the minute I saw it. Then I told the real estate agent that I liked it, and I wanted to ask the owner to adjust the rent. She told me she thought it might not be possible, but that she would call the owner. I felt better just asking her this, because my heart was beating too hard imagining what it would be like to live there.

A few hours later, the real estate agent called me and said that we were approved and that the owner was setting the price as what we needed.

This story is a clear example of the importance of being flexible, listening to our intuition, and believing in it. All the time my mind was saying that I was being completely reckless. First of all, I was going somewhere unknown; secondly, I was asking for a list of extremely expensive houses and then going on to see them; and thirdly, I was asking for a discount on the rent of thirty percent. Well, fortunately I did what my intuition told me to do. I followed the flow.

When we let ourselves go with the flow and we listen to our intuition, we allow what surround us to flow in the right direction. How can we believe in our intuition and allow God to guide us? Allow the flow to take you; it is not necessary to row against the stream. You will see results!

Practice, Practice, Practice

Learning to believe in our intuition is an art. As when you begin painting, or dancing, or doing any sport, you must practice to improve. You must be willing to make mistakes and fail. Remember it takes time to hear your intuition.

You must be willing to take the risk, act on what you are feeling, and learn what works and what doesn't. If you fail, do not be afraid. It is not easy to know which one is the voice of intuition when there are so many voices we hear in our minds. We have ancient voices of childhood memories, others' opinions, fears, doubts, our own mind's voices, and "good ideas."

Notice what happens when you follow your intuition. You will usually feel your energy and power increase, and you will feel things start to flow.

A very important step in hearing and following your intuition process is to practice regularly, at least twice a day.

What's Next?

Good, you have finished reading this book. What is the next step?

Reading a book about personal growth is a huge step, but it will not be the only one you will take. Remember to follow the instructions daily and to re-read the book at least one more time until you make it a part of your life. The next time you feel awkward or as though something is not coming as you wanted it to, try one of the exercises introduced to you.

Sometimes you will feel you are going nowhere. Remember this is a process and each person is going at his or her own pace. It may mean some work at the beginning, but with practice you will get through it.

There is no activity that will not get easier with constant practice. There will come a day when you will feel your life flowing and you will be surprised at what you have accomplished.

Just like your body needs different vitamins and nutrients to work, your life also needs different techniques to grow. Remember, we are a combination of four aspects working in harmony.

Take 5 minutes to pray every day. Feed your body, eat a lot of colorful fruits, drink 8 glasses of water a day. Nourish your attitude, practice positive affirmations - shout them in front of the mirror. Do whatever makes you happy. Open your heart, forgive others, and, above all, forgive yourself.

*Keep this book with your belongings, come to it every time
you feel you need to.*

Years after I graduated with an MBA, I found my purpose in life. I do what I want every day, because I am clear about my intentions and reflect that in my reality every day.

I work from home, where I have a spectacular view of the ocean. I deal with client in different parts of the world. I dedicate special time to my husband, my children, and, of course, to myself. I make time to exercise, eat well, meditate, talk with my angels, and help the world achieve emotional balance and happiness.

My path was not something that developed over night. It is a path which I keep forging and growing with every step I take. As your path unfolds, I'm certain that you will find huge surprises along the way.

God bless you,

Alexandra Navarro, Founder of The Blue Leaf

Blue Leaf
conscious leadership and wellness

The Blue Leaf is dedicated to empowering people, improve their well-being and create optimal perfomance at home and in the workplace.

Our training programs enable people to experience an integral transformational balance at physical, mental, emotional, and spiritual levels.

We believe that a sustainable society begins within each person. Allow us to be part of your journey towards a better way of life.

visit us @
www.theblueleaf.com

Element	Location	Relationship	Block	Question	Actions
Earth	Base of the spine	Survivor	"Freedom secure"	What do you fear the most?	1. Let your fears be displayed clearly 2. Leave fears flow
Water	Lower part of the abdomen	Pleasure	Guilt "Forgive"	Why do you blame yourself?	1. Accept the reality 2. The past can't cloud your life 3. Forgive yourself
Fire	Stomach	Willpower	Shame	What are you ashamed of? When did you disappoint yourself?	1. Do not deny who you are
Wind	Heart	Love	Grief	Have you suffered many losses?	1. The love of God is in your heart 2. Let out all your grief
Sound	Throat	Truth	Lies	Have you lied? Have you told many lies to yourself?	1. Accept your nature
Light	Center of the forehead	Insight	Illusion	Do you think you're separate from others?	1. Everything is connected. Open your mind and accept that things that you think are separate are in fact part of the same.
Thought	Crown of the head	Awareness of all actions	Earthly attachment	Who attaches you to this world?	1. Release these links, let them flow 'orget them.